WAIT

Wilson Oryema

CONTENTS

This is a book about Consumption…

and its far-reaching effects.

Things

The Acquisition, flow, and use of things.

— Consumption

To consume is to deplete and replenish.

What happens when the seafloor disappears amidst a sheet of synthetic polymers?

U . P . C . Y . C . L . E .

One more release
One more colour way

Everyone said it was "must have"

So, of course, I bought a pair

My next post should make 'em salivate
Maybe for a day or two

Until someone remakes the same old shoe
But, this time in blue

So, of course, I will be ready to upload that too

— Chasing the rabbit

Be yourself.

"We are what we eat (consume)"

— Or at least we think we are

The sharing and leasing economy.

— Things to embrace and move towards

Would they from the "old days" consume as much as me if our positions were swapped?

— The answer is probably "yes"

Question — "What is the problem with our consumption?"

Our addictive behaviours will only lead to our destruction. Having us. Gasping. For. Air. Like. A. Fish. That's been hooked out of the water.

Or better yet…

The fish that can't eat.
Because the microplastic it thought was algae.
Is now clogging up its organs.

You are not what you wear.
Separate. From. It.

— This reminded me of that India Arie song, "I am not my hair"

The struggle to separate can be long and arduous, or quick and easy, or you may choose not to at all. All that is for you to determine.

We. Love. Things.

I. Love. Things.

To the point, they become part of our being. And we of theirs.

As we live. They live.

As they live. We live.

As they die. Part of us is taken with them.
As we die. Part of them is taken with us.

R . E . U . S . E .

In Sumere…

The young, rarely ever strive for peace of mind
The old, all they ever want is peace of mind
The haves, think "everybody wants a piece of mine"
And the have-nots, "when will I ever get a piece of mine"

Yet, somehow everybody has the latest fashion accessory, a luxury sofa, and some type of smart device.

And at night, if you listen hard, you can hear last years wants being uploaded to eBay, or thrown out of a speeding car.

These include memory foam mattresses, to trainers that never gained ground, an imitation Eames, and a selfie bulb that was never unbound.

Now, on to the broad description…

It seems the wealth of Sumere isn't measured by the latest trinkets made or up for sale, but rather by the items we carelessly dispel.

A lot is told through the rubbish on the street and the food that's going stale..
(you smell it?)

And the speed it increases at as well!
(you hear it?)

So, anyone that really thought about it. Would wonder if it was really greed, desire, and the hunger for more?

And not stress release, self-care, and to avoid "looking poor".

Either way…

The bin men will be waiting to clean every step of filth,
Celebrated like Santa Claus on December the 25th,
Silently respected as they get to their scheduled shift,
Because nobody wants to do what they do…

Spend time, knee deep in the items nobody wants to remember.

But aren't we all sick of this?
The trash, the consumption, and the lack of fear of consequence.

—— In Sumere 1

The road sweepers bring everybody peace of mind.
Saving the streets from old magazines, to the leftover pizza
slice.

But somehow nobody wonders where they've come from,
where they go, and how they get rid of it all.
Nor where they dump 'em, how it grows, and will we ever
get a whiff of it all?

Surely it will come to a head,
Is it buried deep underground,
Piled high into mountains,
Smouldered to a crisp,
Or pushed out to an archipelago?

Either way…

Something is afoot,
As the city expands wider and wider,
And still, we have yet to come into contact with our
previous desires.

— In Sumere 2

The expansion and more trash mean the disposal team travel further,
Out of town to get rid ~~our~~/their burdens,

Finding new methods to dispose of…
Among other things…

Last years curtains,
A pet rock,
And a shake weight,

As well as, an old game console,
A free umbrella from a magazine,
And a broken up bookcase.

Of course, there's a lot there that shouldn't be their problem,
And they know it too,
As they bemoan to the skies,

"Why do they find recycling such a problem?"

However, with more produced daily than the recycling plants were made to take,
What happens to the extra parts they cannot place,
We know it doesn't disappear into the night…

So, the question becomes whose blame is it to take?

Or should we all just try and do better?

Meanwhile, as they debate who deserves the blame,
Decades go by and engineering excels,
The quality of items increases,
And so does the quantity of trash as well.

Piled higher and higher,
These near-indestructible items,
Now surround the city,
Like a chain of mountains.

— In Sumere 3

As Sumere is renewed every day,
And it's thrown out what it gave value to yesterday,
It presents a conundrum…

How does it preserve itself?

Really, we already know the answer

Through those same items, it has thrown out,
And the ones from the day before,
And the day before that,
And all the things it's discarded over the years, decades,
centuries…

Which in totality, could blanket the world. If not for the
disposal teams of other cities pushing their own trash
further out too.

Now if looking from a distance,
We can see each city,
Surrounded by waste,
And as a result hostile to one another.

As the piles grow larger,
And each city's trash supports the other,
The potential of an avalanche looms further,

Sumere would not escape this,
It would be buried for certain,
Under an immeasurable pile of…
Off trend clothes,
Corroding devices,
And probably some old curtains.

And there Sumere would disappear, consumed by that which was meant to never return.

Along with more things from the past of surrounding cities. Who are all ready to move forward and push down the sordid remains. So, that they can enable their own street cleaners to dispose of more things further and further away.

— In Sumere 4

Could the prayers of the people be heard over their unrelenting desires?

— If they were in fact different

The "clock" is ticking.

R . E . C . Y . C . L . E .

FOR SALE: "Ugh, I saw someone wearing this on the bus."

FOR SALE: "I read somewhere, it was out of fashion"

I heard a funny fact.

There's a tonne of plastic garbage for every person on earth…

Yep.

Funny…

Improvement usually comes step by step.
Not necessarily in large spurts.

It's non-biodegradable.

Virtually indestructible,
If kept away from an in-use crucible.

When they look back at it,
It won't be, to lust at its assets,
But rather to assess our lust for assets,
Of things mostly made from plastic,
Which had us as asses,
Who almost destroyed the planet.

Destroy and Rebuild.

— Cycles

To hide embarrassment?

Or

To protect the babies?

— avoiding the bigger issues

"The 'Devil' finds work for idle hands"

— There's always time to turn it around

The blame game seldom solves anything in the long run

What has happened has already happened

What happens tomorrow, however…

Whether human initiated,
Or solar cycles.

The Planet falling ill,
Or alien outsiders.

Climate change is still happening.

— What it is

Landfills are where rubbish is buried underground…

Will it decompose?
Will it fossilise?
Will leachate leak into aquifers?

Many have these thoughts and questions…

Does daily cover deliver us from infection?
Are the rising gases stopped by our intervention?
And we should care to question, can the local flora and
fauna recover from the disruption?

But there might not be a need to worry…
Things change don't they?

It could be found by future generations,
And for them, I wonder what will come to mind…

— If our seeds make it

Why don't we plant more trees?

Water isn't wet.

— by the way

A two-ton whale washed ashore with 30 plastic bags in its stomach.
It couldn't swallow anything, its organs were obstructed.
Its muscles and fat had thinned, which led to much discussion…

The cause of death?
It was put down, as there was nothing that could be done.

A reverse of health wasn't an option with this one, so the local authorities put a halt to its pain and agony, and made sure it was made to rest in its place of happiness.

— The sea

The microplastics made it into our food and tap water…

They also feed on you and me.

The dirtiest.

The plastic tax.

— Let's make this a thing.

Plastic bags should cost at least 100 times their current price, if not banned completely.

Christmas day is almost over,
I've lost interest in most of my gifts,
These ties and socks… revoltingly kitsch,
And my smile… overly stiff.

The DVDs I received,
I'd already bootlegged & watched for free,
A month ago in fact,
On my phone & smart TV,
Which have run their course,
It's been six months since both were bought.

So off I go,
In my diesel drive,
Cutting through the silence,
Deep into the night,
To find, myself in some items,
Sold at a bargain price.

— Boxing Day Blues Part 1

Looking forward to a diesel-free time.

— Gas guzzlers :/

The half-eaten food
Mixed in with
The used wrapping paper
Mixed in with
The now obsolete items
Mixed in with
The new gifts' packaging
Mixed in with
The receipts we'll regret throwing away

— How to make a Boxing Day bin bag // Boxing Day
Blues Part 2

"Single Use" Plastics…

— why?

Stuffed bodies squeezing from all angles,
Morning breath on the nape may cause me to faint,
Or projectile into this packed crowd.

Either way,
Some personal space would be acquired.

However,
That would hold me up,
So I held it down.

— Black Friday 1

It's my third year here,
The first I got a 36-inch TV,
The following year I got a 42,

This time the 58 with 4k,
and a bent screen…
Is what I'd like to receive,
But we'll have to wait and see.

I've been waiting for a while now…
Maybe next year I should bring my seed.

— Black Friday 2

The murmurs start to dissipate,
The shutters begin to rise.

Conversations of the physical kind,
Begin to break out.
I'm beginning to feel like a corn grain in a frying pan.

Anywho…

Maybe I minced my words earlier.

However,
These elbows will crush and prod,
And my far-reaching arms will clear the way.

Knees in the kidneys for anyone who obstructs me,
And maybe much worse if you're really unlucky.

— Black Friday 3

My victory confirmed,
TV strapped to the car,

And then,
Installation,
As the family grin from afar.

Maybe I should be satisfied…

But,
Since I unloaded my new screen,
I've had thoughts of the following year,
And the next TV for me.

— Black Friday 4

Speeding across the city of big lights and bigger shadows,
Pollution is excessive…
Very far from being green,
Smoke covers the city well like a three-man screen,
Now there's a segment on the radio for how to go green,
And it involves dimming the lights and sitting in shadows…

— Couriers dilemma 1

For me, I cannot care,

I do not have the luxury,

Do they know the struggle of working every day but barely having enough to eat,

Of having a saver menu for lunch and for dinner having to go to sleep,

Either way, it does not matter if they do or don't know,

So off I go into the night, with packages in tow.

— Couriers Dilemma 2

I visit all types of people,
Who order all types of things,
Many in necessity,
And some as a hobby.

Mr. A orders 6 things a week,
And returns 3 or 4,
Mrs. B orders 10,
And returns 7 or more.

I'm always intrigued
And they're always happy to describe,
The items that take up my time,
And lead them to smile.

— Couriers Dilemma 3

Books,
Toiletries,
Holiday-themed clothes,
A toy plane,
A 6-inch nose,
And some leek rolls.

Vuvuzelas,
Air fresheners,
A plastic propeller,
That broke after one spin,
But, was listed as "indestructible".

"Haven't you had enough of this?"
I sometimes wonder,
But who am I to question it,
They pay my shifts…

Albeit barely, because everybody's out for a bargain. Plus, my "employer" encourages this, which for them means razor thin margins.

And for me, means I'm brought on as self-employed, where the minimum wage isn't required, where health insurance and petrol aren't provided. So if I fall sick and can't get cover, I'm the one getting invoiced by the company and charged for cover.

To be honest. I feel smothered.

— Fees & Damages // Couriers Dilemma Part 4

"The customer is always right."

— Or so they say

"Find yourself at our store!"

— Ad

The smile of a child on receiving several pairs of clothing and trainers for a total of £15, and the parent who enabled it…

The bargain trench coat for only a fiver…

The several pairs of socks for a few coins…

— etc. I

The work shirt that fell apart after 20 washes…

The shoe sole that fell off after a month or so…

The favourite tee that lost its shape…

— etc. II

The sound of several thousand sewing machines in unison being fiddled with by overworked and slightly malnourished hands

The extremely cheap clothes we gorge ourselves on, which provide a bright light of "options" for us to choose from, also cast an extensively long shadow, under which isolated communities around the world are subjected to appalling conditions, in order for us to get our items at "bargain" prices.

— An argument for fair pay

Do felines really have nine lives?
Is a lemur's tail striped?
Is this a simulation?
Are we headed for early demise?

I don't know,
These are just some interesting questions,
To bring some attention,
To our worsening condition.

Our town is a pigsty,
A dump for the "rich guys",
Who come from overseas,
To dump PCs and weave lies,

About how they feed the kids,
And eradicate "mean guys",
About how they home the home homeless,
And plant many tree types.

But meanwhile,
I'm chest deep in the dirt,
It's hard to see clear skies,
The burning trash produces smog that reaches upwards of
three miles.

But friend…

I'm not here to ask for a £2 donation,
Or ask you to help me feed mine.

But to tell you.

The problems will reach your shores,
As soon as there's no space on mine.

— Message from a friend who came to me in a dream

Please. wake. up.

Close your eyes…

Imagine massive dead zones,
in oceans across the world,
Filled with chemical sludge,
where our broken down plastics float.

Into the mouths and gills,
Then intestines and rest of the body,
Of unsuspecting sea creatures,
Where they lodge themselves,
Like a parasite,
Waiting for who knows what…

Until its host…
Sinks to the seafloor,
Is washed ashore,
Or becomes dinner.

But through all that,
the plastics,
they survive,
ready to float for a few thousand years more.

— It actually exists

The North Atlantic Garbage Patch.

The North Pacific Garbage Patch.

The Southern Pacific Garbage Patch.

The Indian Ocean Garbage Patch.

— and many more, much smaller and unaccounted for

The pollution sits softly atop everything in the city, almost as if it wasn't there…

— That which you can't see

The flowers can barely breathe.

— and the same goes for me

Overpopulation
Is
An
Overcrowded
Cities
Problem

.

And
A
Distribution
One

,
Too

.

On the twelfth day of Christmas, my true love gave to me,

An
Assortment
Of
Things
I
Will
Quickly
Lose
Interest
In
.

Consumption isn't just what you eat and buy.

— Reiterating the first page

Nothing exists in a vacuum.

— Ripples

There's a split from here.

Others

Lifestyles and narratives

— Things we consume (For better or worse)

Friendships and partners

— Other things we consume

Our consumption habits.
Tell us a lot.
About.
Where we've come from.
And.
Where we are most likely going.

— If going by Evolutionary Biology and Psychology

Even our addictions can be pinned down to a mixture of mostly inherited and some environmental factors.

— Addiction is an extreme form of consumption

Loving (or rather obsessing) over someone to the point you want to control their actions, thoughts, and/or emotions is the first step onto a very slippery slope.

— Abuse

Of course, you wanted all of me,
I gave you life,
But, I'm not yours to keep,
Nor are you for me.

— Let me soar

Does addiction become an addiction when you consume more of something than typically "socially acceptable" or when it becomes a risk to yours or others personal well being?

When you're surrounded by all you want and need. but. still. you're missing something.

— The feeling when...

Fear.

Self-loathing.

Extreme loneliness.

Stressors encourage more consumption.

— imbalances

"This thing is so me!"

— as were the 99 things before it

"I just had to get it…"

"You would've done the same if you were in my position"

Food manufacturers make more from the food we leave on the plate as opposed to the food that goes into our stomachs.

— Old wives tales

How do you expect me to curb my addictions?
The ones publicly condemned.
When we receive cues all day.
To encourage those habits once again.

— Advertising

How much do you consume in order to better relate to others?

Keep scrolling. Keep scrolling.

You have 400 new notifications…

Keep scrolling. Keep scrolling.

"Over 30 people in your area have won this year, find out how you can be next!"

Keep scrolling. Keep scrolling.

"This $10 cream will put an end to your back pain forever!"

Did you see what happened to?
Did you check so & so's latest post?

No…?!

You're missing out, man
You should really check your phone

I mean……

What else is there to do?

Does the sky ever stop being blue?
Will the concrete you walk on tell you about who just
made a couture thong?

No?

Then what better do you have to do…
Oh, and subscribe to me too!

— FOMO (Fear Of Missing Out)

In the future,
It is said,
And hoped by many,
That virtual reality will evolve to the point that,
We will live in matrix-esque pods,
From where,
We will be able to communicate to everyone,
Complete any given tasks,
Or desires,
And consume anything and everything
From the comfort of said pod.

— Why would we ever leave

Full of potential,
Now running on empty,
Left to leak,
As if a bowl with a hole in the middle.

Now every chance he gets he piddles,
And not down a back alley,
Nor a kitchen sink,
But on his own chances, hopes, and dreams.

— Lost part 1

How is it,
That it comes to this,
That one destined for heights,
Can't escape his pit,
Has overindulged on life,
Plus his brain's been nicked,
And now looks like something death has kissed?

Fear.

It could box you in,
Have you rip off the packaging,
Or mixed with pressure,
Have you running away from many challenges.

I mean..

Even meeting friends,
Leaving the house for lunch,
And appearing online,
Could feel like you've been forced to jump.

— Lost part 2

This message is brought to you by someone who used to drink fear from a 30-gallon soda can. Was smothered by pressure to the point for anything he never thought "he can". And used to cry himself to sleep in hopes that he would maybe drown.

— Lost part 3

It's cool to love things,
But be you,
On your own.

It doesn't matter,
If you have the latest trainer,
Or mobile phone.

Always looking over others shoulders,
On what to covet,
Or who to be,
Will have you with no place for your own,
And staring blankly at a brightly lit screen,
From dawn till dusk,
Or at least until you need to pee.

— Lost part 4

But if not,
It sounds great!

I'm sure the cool points, trends, and likes,
Will physically and spiritually feed you.
So that your own interests and self-development won't
need to.

Anyway…

That's enough for me,
I'm sure I'm getting on your nerves,
Because from your view,
I probably look like another caged bird.

— Lost part 5

Are we destabilising our children from an early age with an endless supply of things and ever increasingly shinier objects?

— Sincerely yours

Giving in to their every whim…

But who says we can control our own?

— Desires

Do you savour every aspect, or eat hurriedly to start sooner on the next one?

— Consuming relationships

She likened herself to a kid in a candy store.
But a sweet tooth is rarely a good thing.

— Sugar Crash

Was I…
Too sweet
Too bitter
Hard to chew
Or swallowed all too easily

"The way to one's heart is through their stomach"

And fast food will take its toll on your body…

Even the most jagged rock,
Can taste like it was picked from Eden.

If we lose touch with our senses.

— First Bite

I take up all your time,
But you,
Not a second of mine,
And that's…
Not by coincidence.

I want to go to the beach.
I need to be wined and dined.

Or gin if you've got some…

It takes two to tango,
And maybe no one truly wants to eat alone,
But at my table,
Don't touch my food,
And send yours along too.

How can we bring food to the table and you eat it all?
You know I love my vegetables,
And also your sundries.

But what use is us dining together,
If you're the only one,
Who gets to try,
And what use are the sides and condiments,
If they have nothing to compliment.

The breadsticks and the olives aren't enough,
The only thing they leave me with,
Is a salty taste in my mouth,
And nothing to wash it down.

I'm dying of thirst.

We found a new spring.
The oil looks and tastes like water.
And swallows all in its path somewhat like it too.

— A dark embrace

S
Se
Sea
Sear
Searc
Search
Search.
Search. F
Search. Fi
Search. Fin
Search. Find
Search. Find.
Search. Find. U
Search. Find. Us
Search. Find. Use
Search. Find. Use.
Search. Find. Use. R
Search. Find. Use. Re
Search. Find. Use. Rep
Search. Find. Use. Repe
Search. Find. Use. Repea
Search. Find. Use. Repeat
Search. Find. Use. Repeat.

— Chasing the "tail"

Do you drown yourself in others in hopes to fill that which you think is "missing" in yourself?

— Confidence

And breathe.

I spent hours and years searching for it, and when I had an ounce of it in my hand, I tossed it aside and kept running forward, in hopes of more…

It took me a while to realise…
Even a drop.
Could keep me quenched.
For an eternity.

The final turn.

Narratives

We are often led to consume narratives purely by the surrounding beings and objects which operate as if said narrative is true.

— …

When I was young,
I was confused…

As I was told,
I only had 500 years of history.

— What a time to be alive

How old do you think the planet is?

I have this thing I do every so often, where I ask friends and other people I randomly meet:
How old do they think the planet earth is?

At first, I expected to get answers within a specific range, but the responses varied massively and were underpinned by a very different set of beliefs. I won't go into their reasonings here but the numbers (ages) that were given to me include:

"4,000 years"

"10,000 years"

"20,000 years"

"100,000 years"

"A few million years"

"A few billion years"

"Whatever the carbon dating says"

"The last possible number"

"We've always been here…"

Query: I'm suffering from a slight headache, wheezing, and a bump on my arm?

Search results: From what we gather you may have one of the following — cancer, tuberculosis, yellow fever, dengue fever, mumps, rash, flu, cold, or a fever.

— Search engines

The preacher told me, "fish and loaves" are what the gospel said.

The doctor told me to "balance it out" and eat bits of everything instead.

My spot at the gym told me to eat "protein heavy" as it'll be good for gains.

And my friend suggested whatever "would not cause me pain."

— Diets

My subscriptions box is full of people each telling me in their own way how I can get ripped in 21 days

Somehow, without my name, size, age, height, diet, or body type…

Sensational…

"It makes for a good story…"

Insert MILDLY (or COMPLETELY) INACCURATE and CONTROVERSIAL HEADLINE here

"It could be the next '-gate'"

The story (his or hers) changes each time the message is passed along.

— The telephone game as a metaphor for life

All is fair in the war for attention.

"Alternative facts"

The modern concept of "race" was created in order to isolate and disadvantage particular groups of people based on their heritage and appearance, and bind them to a never-changing lowly status socially, economically, politically, and educationally. While other groups were propped up and provided with access to unlimited power and wealth.

Many individuals and organisations including the American Anthropological Association all support the evidence that "race" has no biological basis. And even within these particular groups, there are more biological variations inside of them than when compared to other groups.

The cultural and behavioural markers groups have had assigned to them have been fabricated to propagate false beliefs and agendas.

— For a full breakdown read the "AAA statement on race"

How many wars have been started because of it…

How many people have died because of it…

How many families have been broken apart…

Sigh.

"Be hard.
Not soft.
Don't cry. It's weak.
If they see you cry, you've lost.
Encourage physicality.
Be vengeful. Not merciful.
It's all about the size of your 'cojones'.
YOU HAVE TO PLAY A SPORT.
Compete.
Your clothes and hair must be masculine.
Flex your muscles from time to time.
Make sure you're the strongest.
Don't be a "sissy". (Whatever that means)
Be aggressive.
Winning is the only thing that counts.
Blood. Sweat. Tears.
Be forceful.
Always compete."

—— Weird things asked of young men // Toxic

Who told you to hold back your tears?
Let them heal you.

— A message to my teenage self

Filter.

When I was just a little girl,
I had dreams of what I could be,
But, before my wishes,
Could take on a form,
Here's what was said to me…

"Life is hard my dear,
Please marry before your 33rd year,
Or things will look bleak and weird…
Farewell, my dear!"

— Whatever you will 1

I was a slightly older girl,
When I was taught,
Of the birds and the bees,
So, as well as my marriage,
And to be a good spouse,
Here's what was asked of me…

"Have some kids, my dear,
Preferably by 30 years,
Or you'll be a failure to me,
And the rest of society."

— Whatever you will 2

Now I have kids of my own,
They ask me many things,
Like what they will be,
So, I think back,
To what I was told,
And here's what i said to them…

"Have some fun my dears,
Never be consumed by fear,
Chase after all your dreams,
And be the best you can be."

— Whatever you will 3

Be open.

I turned on the news today,
In town, there was a fray,
I had to turn my head away,
We pray no one dies today.

But as I turn my head away,
To my side, I notice other frays,
Across the world,
In all types of places,
Many lives were lost today.

Also, people being enslaved,
Sold for pennies and enchained,
It really goes on today,
And with no action,
there will be never-ending pain.

And then I think to the people that were slain,
By bullets and bombs from planes,
They won't get a hearse today,
Just a bulldozer to clear the rubble for someone else's gain.

I read a story about the threats overseas,
Each one as heinous as the other.

And how if they ever reached our shores,
We would most likely be smothered.

The cynic in me advises not to trust it,
But I still find myself,
Eyeballs bulged,
Scrolling,
Looking for more updates.

— Sleight of hand 1

Days, Months, Years go by,
My friends,
Warn me of my obsession,
The worry is never sated,
As information is regularly updated.

So, still, I stay fearful,
Wary of that which may still be coming.

Always from the lands of others,
Never that on which I was standing.

But that which propped me up,
And allegedly,
Was here for my protection,
Was, in fact, placing me in an unsuspecting chokehold,
For which,
I had no defences.

— Sleight of hand 2

"Never let a day slip by without agenda"

— Everyone wants to leave a footprint behind

I found myself in the book and took the lessons I NEEDED.

Then I was stopped by Mrs. A and she said I "was in trouble" as I was reading it wrong and "THESE were the lessons I needed".

Mr. G pulled me over shortly after and corrected me by informing me "THESE were the lessons I NEEDED" and told me that everything else was misleading.

I overheard a group shouting in the street and they told me all I required was in the first half and everything else WASN'T needed.

Confused, I spoke to my elder and they said to me "everything isn't for everyone" and she took what SHE needed.

— Misleading

Transparency.

Those who sound like _____ are all _____
Those who smell like _____ are all _____
Those who look like _____ are all _____
Those who live in _____ are all _____
Those who eat _____ are all _____
Those who wear _____ are all _____
Those who drink _____ are all _____
Those who pray to _____ are all _____
Those who have _____ are all _____
Those who don't have _____ are all _____

— Stereotypes // Fill in the blanks

I was always taught to finish my food.
Regardless of the portion.
And show gratitude.
Without critiquing the quality.

Never to…
Signal when in need of a respite.
Or decline when it does not match my appetite.

—— Learning to say no // Becoming a picky eater

Be wary of.
What you consume.
When you consume
How you consume.
Where you consume.

— Etiquette

Thank you for reading.

ACKNOWLEDGEMENTS

In the process of making this book, I have had support
from an endless amount of people. As such, I would like
to thank them but especially the following who helped in
various ways, whether through; general advice, inspiring
me through casual conversation, or reading the earlier
versions and giving much-needed encouragement
whenever I felt I was running on empty!

Special thanks to:
Harley Weir. Marco Cossu. Nat Haynes. Cyrus Jackson.
William Farr. Genevieve Garner. Lucy Kumara Moore.
Victoire Simonney. Kesewa Aboah. Adwoa Aboah.
Tomi Ahmed. Leo Gibbon. Jerome Tamashi.
Athena Paginton. Lynette Nylander. Eva Tausig.
Helen Ralli. Campbell Addy. Nahwand Jaff.
Daniel "Deray" Clarke. Samuel Santos. Maxi.
Paula Karaiskos. Jemil Saka. Kai Gillespie. Millie Kotseva.
All the team at Storm London.

ABOUT THE WRITER

Wilson Oryema is based in London, England. He works across various mediums including, photography, text, and film. His works primarily explore human behaviour and its effects on the planet, through several themes, such as consumption, and aggression.

You can find more of his work at;
www.wilsonoryema.com

Printed in Great Britain
by Amazon